THE ANIMAL FILES
WE NEED
PLANKTON

by Ben McClanahan

WWW.FOCUSREADERS.COM

Focus Readers is distributed by North Star Editions:
sales@northstareditions.com | 888-417-0195

Produced for Focus Readers by Red Line Editorial.

Content Consultant: Emilie Villar, Marine Biologist, The National Center for Scientific Research, France

Photographs ©: RLSPhoto/iStockphoto, cover, 1; Choksawatdikorn/Shutterstock Images, 4–5; Sally Bensusen/NASA EOS Project Science Office/NASA, 7; Robert Simmon and Jesse Allen/NASA, 9; sangriana/Shutterstock Images, 10–11; Rattiya Thongdumhyu/Shutterstock Images, 13 (phytoplankton); Napat/Shutterstock Images, 13 (zooplankton), 14; Zahra22/Shutterstock Images, 13 (small fish); furtseff/Shutterstock Images, 13 (larger fish); Jiang Hongyan/Shutterstock Images, 13 (squid); frantisekhojdysz/Shutterstock Images, 13 (shark); PawelG Photo/Shutterstock Images, 16–17; Geraldo Ramos/Shutterstock Images, 18–19; Chatchai Srisupawadee/Shutterstock Images, 20; Alfred Rowan/Shutterstock Images, 22; ifish/iStockphoto, 24–25; Yurikr/iStockphoto, 27; Richard Whitcombe/Shutterstock Images, 29

Library of Congress Cataloging-in-Publication Data
Names: McClanahan, Ben, 1978- author.
Title: We need plankton / Ben McClanahan.
Description: Lake Elmo, MN : Focus Readers, [2019] | Series: The animal files
   | Audience: Grade 4 to 6. | Includes index.
Identifiers: LCCN 2018038071 (print) | LCCN 2018038550 (ebook) | ISBN
   9781641854863 (PDF) | ISBN 9781641854283 (e-book) | ISBN 9781641853125
   (hardcover) | ISBN 9781641853705 (paperback)
Subjects: LCSH: Plankton--Ecology--Juvenile literature. |
   Plankton--Conservation--Juvenile literature.
Classification: LCC QH90.8.P5 (ebook) | LCC QH90.8.P5 M28 2019 (print) | DDC
   577.6--dc23
LC record available at https://lccn.loc.gov/2018038071

Printed in the United States of America
Mankato, MN
October, 2018

ABOUT THE AUTHOR
Ben McClanahan is a writer who enjoys learning about science and nature. He hopes more people learn about the importance plankton play in our daily lives.

TABLE OF CONTENTS

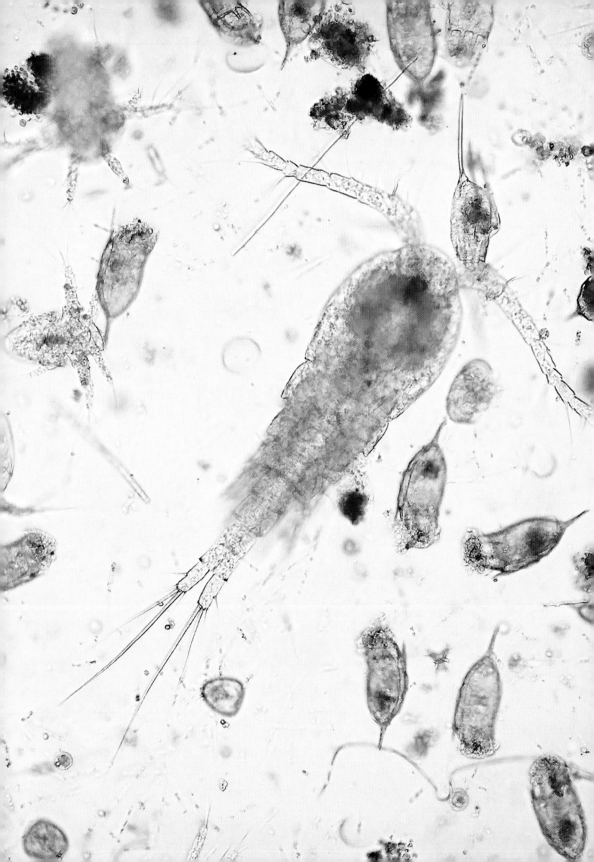

CHAPTER 1

DRIFTERS

In a single spoonful of ocean water, an entire world exists. Plankton are tiny **organisms**. They drift in oceans, rivers, and lakes. Humans can rarely see them. Still, plankton play a huge role on Earth. For example, much of the air that humans breathe depends on plankton. So do many of the foods that humans eat.

Plankton can be seen up close under a microscope.

Even the oil that humans use as fuel comes from ancient plankton.

Most plankton are too small to see. But under a microscope, plankton look like plants and animals. Phytoplankton are one type of plankton. These plankton are similar to plants. They can produce their own food. Other plankton are similar to tiny animals. They feed on other organisms. These ones are called zooplankton.

Plankton get their name from the Greek word *planktos*. In Greek, it means "drifting." Plankton are so small they cannot swim easily. Instead, wind and water move them around.

On their own, plankton are tiny. But they often gather together in huge groups. Groups of plankton often float near the ocean's surface. Phytoplankton take in sunlight, carbon dioxide, and nutrients. As they float, they give off oxygen. In fact, half of all oxygen on Earth comes from plankton.

TYPES OF PHYTOPLANKTON

There are many types of phytoplankton. Below are some of the most common types.

cyanobacteria   diatom   dinoflagellate   green algae   coccolithophore

Plankton also provide food for sea animals. Without plankton, many animals would not exist. Small fish, big fish, and whales eat plankton. Even zooplankton eat phytoplankton to survive.

Plankton are some of the oldest life-forms on Earth. Millions of years ago, plankton sent a burst of oxygen into

PLANKTON FROM SPACE

Some of the best views of plankton come from space. Scientists use **satellites** to study plankton in large numbers. Plankton form groups over huge areas of ocean. Then, light reflects off the plankton. Colorful swirls appear. Images of the swirls help scientists study plankton on a large scale.

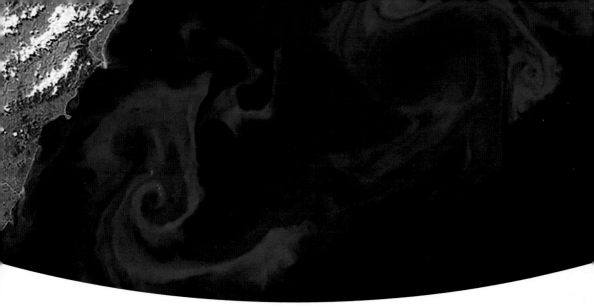

This photo taken from space shows swirls of plankton near New Zealand.

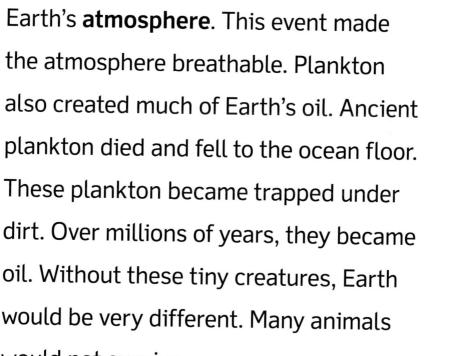

Earth's **atmosphere**. This event made the atmosphere breathable. Plankton also created much of Earth's oil. Ancient plankton died and fell to the ocean floor. These plankton became trapped under dirt. Over millions of years, they became oil. Without these tiny creatures, Earth would be very different. Many animals would not survive.

CHAPTER 2

LUNGS OF THE EARTH

Plankton form the base of the trophic pyramid. This diagram shows how energy moves between organisms. Energy flows through **food chains**. Phytoplankton are at the bottom of many food chains. They are primary producers. This means phytoplankton make their own food.

Plankton form thick layers on lakes, ponds, and other bodies of water.

They create energy by taking in sunlight and carbon dioxide. Then they send oxygen into the air. Phytoplankton are sometimes called the "lungs of Earth." Like lungs, they take in and send out air.

Producers provide food for consumers. Consumers gain energy by eating other organisms. For example, zooplankton are consumers. They eat phytoplankton. Fish are consumers, too. They eat both phytoplankton and zooplankton.

Phytoplankton need sunlight to survive. For this reason, they float near the top of the water. Some animals swim to the surface to eat these plankton. When plankton die, they fall to the ocean floor.

Animals along the bottom eat these dead plankton.

Phytoplankton mainly live along coasts. They also tend to live near the equator.

TROPHIC PYRAMID

The trophic pyramid is made up of producers and consumers. Some consumers are herbivores, which eat plants. Others are carnivores, which eat meat.

Top carnivores (sharks, dolphins)

Third-level carnivorous consumers (squid)

Second-level carnivorous consumers (larger fish)

First-level carnivorous consumers (small fish)

Herbivorous consumers (zooplankton)

Sun's energy

Primary producers (phytoplankton)

Brine shrimp are a type of zooplankton.

There are more nutrients in this part of the world. Winds bring the nutrients to the ocean's surface. Plankton need these nutrients to grow. However, water temperature affects the nutrients. Nutrients often sink in warm water. As a result, there are fewer plankton in the summer.

Phytoplankton grow in the spring. At this time of year, ice melts in cold regions. The melting ice leaves a layer of nutrients. Meanwhile, sunlight breaks through the water. Sunlight helps plankton grow faster. It gives them energy.

OPEN-WATER PLANKTON

Not all plankton live by shores. Bacterioplankton live in open waters. These plankton are a type of **bacteria**. Like all plankton, they live in large groups. Some **species** of bacterioplankton are very old. They have existed for 3.5 billion years. These plankton can survive harsh conditions. They provide food for animals in deep, cold water.

GLOWING PLANKTON

Some plankton light up. These species are similar to fireflies. They contain a specific chemical. When this chemical reacts with oxygen, it produces light.

Dinoflagellates are a type of glowing plankton. These plankton gather in large groups. They form bio bays. A bio bay is a body of water filled with glowing plankton.

Some plankton can be dangerous if eaten. Some dinoflagellates have toxic chemicals. Fish may eat these plankton. Then humans may eat the fish. The chemicals from the plankton can make humans sick.

Plankton light up a beach in the Maldives, an island nation in the Indian Ocean.

CHAPTER 3

LEARNING ABOUT PLANKTON

Scientists need many tools to study plankton. They use nets to collect plankton from water. And they use microscopes to look at plankton up close.

Before 1931, scientists knew very little about plankton. An invention by Alister Hardy changed that. Hardy made the Continuous Plankton Recorder (CPR).

A scientist drags a net through wetlands in Brazil to collect phytoplankton.

Scientists keep plankton samples alive with light and oxygen.

This tool collects plankton samples. Scientists drag the CPR behind a boat. Filters inside the CPR collect the plankton.

The first CPR collected plankton in the North Sea. The study, called the CPR

Survey, has collected samples since 1931. The CPR Survey collects approximately 5,500 samples per year. These samples come from all over the world. They include nearly 800 types of plankton.

Scientists study plankton populations very closely. The number of plankton can affect biodiversity. Biodiversity is the variety of living things in an area. Animals thrive where there is more plankton to eat. But plankton populations can also grow too fast. When this happens, they form an algal bloom. An algal bloom is a thick buildup of **algae**. Some harmful algal blooms are called red tides. During a red tide, plankton turn the water red.

This red tide formed off the coast of South Africa.

Some of these plankton are toxic. They can kill fish. They can also make humans sick.

Algal blooms create dead zones. During a bloom, dead phytoplankton fall to the ocean floor. As they break down, they use up oxygen. This process causes oxygen levels to fall. And when that happens, other animals can die due to the lack of oxygen.

Scientists study algal blooms to predict when dead zones might form. Catching a dead zone early can lower its impact.

FRESHWATER PLANKTON

The study of plankton is not limited to the sea. Scientists also study freshwater plankton. These species live in lakes, ponds, and rivers. Freshwater plankton include algae, diatoms, and flagellates.

CHAPTER 4

PROTECTING PLANKTON

Plankton are some of the oldest forms of life. They have existed for billions of years. However, plankton are in danger. Human activity is threatening them.

One of the biggest threats is **global warming**. When air temperatures rise, water temperatures rise, too. But in warm water, fewer nutrients rise to the surface.

Many animals, such as crabs, rely on plankton for food.

Without these nutrients, phytoplankton cannot grow. And without phytoplankton, there is less food for other animals. For example, falling numbers of plankton can lead to fewer fish.

Phytoplankton populations have been decreasing since 1950. The decline is worst in the Northern Hemisphere. Here, populations have fallen by 40 percent.

In other cases, global warming might cause too much plankton to grow. Due to global warming, water is warming up in cold areas. Plankton that prefer warmer water could move to these areas. That could cause algal blooms to form. These blooms would reduce the amount of food

Warm weather caused plankton to cover a river in Ukraine.

available. Birds and fish would have less to eat. Scientists are studying these changes. However, they still have a lot to learn.

Pollution is another threat to plankton. Along coasts, humans cause nutrient pollution. Water treatment and farming are two examples of nutrient pollution.

They cause waste to seep into the ocean. This waste often contains nutrients. And large amounts of nutrients can lead to harmful algal blooms. Scientists are working to help others understand the risks of pollution.

Plastic is also a threat to plankton. Each year, approximately 5.3 billion pounds (2.4 billion kg) of plastic enter the ocean. Over time, plastic breaks into tiny pieces. Plankton mistake these pieces for food. Then other animals eat the plankton. In this way, plastic can harm entire food chains.

Plankton are important to all forms of life. So, it's important to keep them

Plastic negatively affects marine ecosystems.

healthy. Scientists are looking for new ways to remove plastic from oceans. Meanwhile, families can try to use less plastic. They can also recycle plastic products. Thankfully, plankton are strong organisms. They have **adapted** to changes in the planet for millions of years. They will continue to impact the world.

FOCUS ON
PLANKTON

Write your answers on a separate piece of paper.

1. Write a paragraph summarizing the main ideas of Chapter 3.

2. Would you rather observe plankton under a microscope or from space? Why?

3. What year did Alister Hardy invent the Continuous Plankton Recorder?

   A. 1931
   B. 1950
   C. 1953

4. On a food chain, where are consumers?

   A. above producers
   B. below producers
   C. on the same level as producers

Answer key on page 32.

GLOSSARY

adapted
Changed over time to deal with a certain situation.

algae
Tiny, plant-like organisms that live in water and produce oxygen.

atmosphere
The layers of gases that surround a planet or moon.

bacteria
Single-celled living things. They can be useful or harmful.

food chains
The feeding relationships among different living things.

global warming
A long-term increase in the temperature of Earth's atmosphere caused by rising levels of pollution.

organisms
Various kinds of living things, from plants and animals to single-celled life-forms.

satellites
Objects or vehicles that orbit a planet or moon, often to collect information.

species
Groups of animals or plants that are similar.

TO LEARN MORE

BOOKS

Arlon, Penelope. *Really? Ocean.* New York: Scholastic, 2015.

Pressberg, Dava. *Producers, Consumers, and Decomposers.* New York: PowerKids Press, 2017.

Rowell, Rebecca. *Sylvia Earle: Extraordinary Explorer and Marine Biologist.* Minneapolis: Abdo Publishing, 2016.

NOTE TO EDUCATORS

Visit **www.focusreaders.com** to find lesson plans, activities, links, and other resources related to this title.

INDEX

Answer Key: 1. Answers will vary; **2.** Answers will vary; **3.** A; **4.** A